THEY DIED TOO YOUNG

JOHN LENNON

BY
Tom Stockdale

This edition first published by Parragon Books Ltd in 1995

Produced by
Magpie Books Ltd, London

Copyright © Parragon Book Service Ltd 1995
Unit 13–17, Avonbridge Trading Estate, Atlantic Road
Avonmouth, Bristol, BS11 9QD

Illustrations courtesy of: Rex Features.

ISBN 0 75250 735 4

A copy of the British Library Cataloguing in Publication
Data is available from the British Library.

Typeset by Hewer Text Composition Services, Edinburgh
Printed in Singapore by Printlink International Co.

THEY DIED TOO YOUNG
John Lennon

Early Years

John Lennon was born during an air-raid on 9 October 1940 in a Liverpool that trembled under the nightly German attacks of the Battle of Britain. His life would be one which blew its own winds of change into the growing mass culture of the post-war world, and which, by its innovation and controversy, will stand as an example of personal striving and musical excellence for much longer than the forty years which he lived.

John's mother Julia gave him the patriotic middle name 'Winston', and struggled to bring him up while her husband Freddie was at sea with the merchant navy. By the time Freddie returned in November 1944, Julia had met a Welsh soldier and was pregnant by him, and had left baby John with his uncle. The new baby was adopted, and Freddie brought John back and tried to patch up the marriage. However, the attractive Julia had fallen for another man, John Dykins, and moved in with him in 1946.

So John's early life was one of instability, and his character soon showed the results: he was thrown out of his infant school for misbehaviour. His despairing father had gone back to sea, believing that there was no hope for a family life, and didn't know that John had been farmed out to Julia's sister, Mimi. Mimi, a model of propriety, became the rock in John's life, but her strictness was a source of contention for the aggressive child. He was forced into the confines of the middle-class culture which his aunt planned for him, though her husband George would sometimes manage to slip him into a Western at the local cinema. His enforced loneliness made him the centre of his own world, and the combination of aggression and ego helps to explain much of the trouble that his quick tongue caused later on.

At school, he suffered from undiagnosed dyslexia, an affliction which was in some ways a gift, for it brought a quirky style to his literary work. His teachers were more concerned with his bad manners, stealing and bullying of other pupils at Dovedale Primary School, where he was at the head of an unruly gang of boys. By the time he moved on to Quarry Bank Grammar School in September 1952 his neighbourhood knew who the likely culprit was if a firework went off through their letter-box, or their daughters came home crying from school.

From about this time John recovered his relationship with his mother, whom he found a fun-loving alternative to the dictatorial Mimi. The brooding anger of *Rebel Without a Cause* and the explosion of rock 'n' roll that Bill Haley brought to Britain in 1955 was perfect for the rebellious youth, who was soon dressing as a Teddy boy. Julia's home was a base from which he was allowed more freedom, especially after the death of George, Mimi's husband. Julia was accepting of John's first serious girl-friend, and bought him his first guitar after the effect of Elvis Presley's 'Heart-break Hotel' gave him the musical itch. The country was rocking to the touring bands from America, like Fats Domino, Eddie Cochran and, one of Lennon's big influences, Little Richard. The inspiration of Lonnie Donnegan was behind the growth of skiffle bands around the country, and the sixteen-year-old Lennon followed suit in 1957 with his first band, the Quarrymen (named after Quarry Bank School, which most of the band attended).

The Quarrymen played a gig on 6 July 1957 where Lennon was introduced to James Paul McCartney. Although he was a year younger than John, Paul was a better guitar player and impressed Lennon with a rendition of Eddie Cochran's 'Twenty Flight Rock' to get himself a place in the band. Paul wanted a friend of his, George Harrison, to join the Quarrymen but Harrison was only fourteen, and although he proved his guitar skills, Lennon would not let him join for a year.

The Quarrymen were together until 1959, when they imploded in arguments and a final drunken fight, giving them no chance of emulating the likes of Cliff Richard and Adam Faith at the top of the charts. By this time Mimi had got

John into Liverpool College of Art by the skin of his teeth, for he had failed all his O levels. His new style was the thin black look of the beatnik, which stood out amongst the duffle-coats, and he carried his disruptive tactics from the classroom into the art studio, where the nudity of the life classes was an obvious target; he was not allowed into the painting department in his second year. Meanwhile, McCartney and Harrison were studying at the Liverpool Institute next door, and the three would play and sing through lunch and break-times. John and Paul agreed early on that they would be credited as a partnership on any songs that they wrote, together or separately.

Lennon's behaviour became even less stable after the death of his mother in 1958. She was run over by an off-duty policeman without a driving licence, who received only a reprimand and suspension as a punishment. John started to drink heavily and his bullying became more violent, as he would pick on anyone in the bar he happened to be in. His hurtfulness and cynicism were the only defence he had against the vulnerability that he felt.

Lennon had started going steady with Cynthia Powell, a fellow art student. Her parents were very much against their relationship, but Cynthia believed she could bring out his gentle side. By this time, assured of failing his exams, he had moved into the flat of his friend

Stuart Sutcliffe, to form a new band around himself, Paul and George. Sutcliffe, a talented art student, gave up his studies when offered the bass player's job, and it was he who came up with a name for the band, after the motorbike gang from the film *The Wild One*, the Beetles. It also gave a nod to Buddy Holly's Crickets, and was given a rhythmic slant by Lennon, turning the 'beet' into 'beat' and the Beetles into the Beatles.

What The World Was Waiting For

By 1960 Britain was full of Elvis clones, with Cliff Richard at their head, and the softer rock of Roy Orbison and Ritchie Valens was coming over from America. Liverpool had the advantage of a port in that a wider range of American imports came into the docks – the original Black singers from whom Elvis learned his trade, like Joe Turner or Willa Mae Thornton. The Liverpool scene was one of cheap dance nights and running gang battles, and the Silver Beatles, as they were called for a while, found it hard to get a gig behind tough rock 'n' roll outfits like Cass and the Cassanovas. However, a good performance in the presence of talent-spotter Larry Parnes got them a short tour of Scotland backing one of Parnes's finds, Johnny Gentle. The Beatles' drummer, Tommy Moore, pulled out of the band after the tour, so the rest of the band tried to persuade Pete Best to leave his band, the Blackjacks. He was won over by the Beatles' chance to go to Hamburg. Allan Williams, club and coffee bar owner, had already sent a couple of bands to play in some of the red-light clubs out there, and, in August 1960, he got the Beatles a residency at the Club Indra.

The Cavern Club, one of the Beatles'
first venues

The Beatles at the height of Beatlemania

It took only one performance in front of the drunken crowds of the Hamburg strip-joint for the band to realize that just standing and singing was not going to go down well. They quickly learned how to draw an audience with on-stage antics and rowdy behaviour which they kept up during draining seven-hour sets. Soon the band was receiving crates of beer, thrown onto the stage, and were as legless as the audience.

They returned to Hamburg in the spring of 1961, playing at the Top Ten Club, where the party continued. Sex was as available as beer, and nightly orgies would take place with any number of girls. The only danger for them in those days was the clap, and, as John commented after catching it, 'One shot in the butt, and it was gone'. So sex and alcohol, along with preludin 'pep pills', were the spindle around which Lennon's life revolved, and he learned to function in a drunken haze. Stuart Sutcliffe, on the other hand, fell in love with a German, Astrid Kircherr, and soon left the band to be with her, and return to his art.

Back in Liverpool, with the advantage of their experience in Germany, the Beatles found it easy to get gigs in the low-ceilinged basement of a warehouse called the Cavern Club. With an exciting show and wealth of material they were soon a popular attraction, and a version of 'My Bonnie' that they recorded with singer Tony Sheridan was in demand at the NEMS record shop, run by Brian Epstein. Intrigued by a single that was outselling established bands, he made what would be the first of many visits to the Cavern in October 1961, and became infatuated by the band – more, as popular legend has it, through lust than business acumen. In January 1962 he became their manager, although he would be learning this new trade as he went along. By then the Beatles had been voted top group by Liverpool's *Mersey Beat* magazine.

In April 1962 the Beatles were headlining at Hamburg's Star Club, though they were met at the airport with the bombshell of Stuart Sutcliffe's death from a brain haemorrhage, resulting from a fight some months previously. The Star Club residencies proved the making of the Beatles, although John's behaviour worsened with Sutcliffe's death, and included walking the streets in his underwear and pelting nuns with water-filled condoms.

On 1 January the band had made a demo for Decca which became a musical millstone around the neck of its A&R man, Dick Rowe, when he rejected it. The tape found its way to George Martin at EMI, who gave them a session in June. His dissatisfaction with the drumming of Pete Best was instrumental in the latter being replaced with the plainer face but more stable beat of Richard Starkey, or Ringo Starr. Martin was wary of allowing the band to do their own material, but it was a McCartney song, 'Love Me Do', which became their first single. The second, 'Please Please Me', a Lennon composition, evoked the producer's response: 'Gentlemen, you've just made your first number one record.'

In between the recording of 'Please Please Me' and the confirmation of George Martin's prophecy in February 1963, Lennon got married to the pregnant Cynthia on 23 August, and the band recorded an album during one night in the middle of a nationwide tour. From the opening notes of 'I Saw Her Standing There' to the closing chords of 'Twist And Shout', the Beatles laid down a fresh, raw and very English adaptation of the American rock which grabbed their audiences, giving them the headlining role on a tour in March, and beginning a songwriting roller-coaster which turned the world upside down.

Beatlemania

On 8 April 1963, Cynthia Lennon gave birth to a son, John Charles Julian. The child did not meet his father for a week, and this lack of contact became the pattern in Julian Lennon's life. John was in the first flush of stardom, and was not only very busy, but also disinclined to admit to the mundanity of family duty. His marriage was hidden from the world for eighteen months, during which time his lifestyle was very much that of a bachelor. He continued to suffer fits of drunken violence, beating up DJ Bob Wooler at Paul's twenty-first birthday party for a remark which John took to be a slur on his relationship with Brian Epstein. John's change of character under various influences was something for his closest friends to be wary of.

The instant influence of the Beatles is obvious from the album charts of 1963. *Please Please Me* took the number one spot from Cliff Richard's *Summer Holiday* in May and relinquished it only to *With the Beatles* in December, as part of a full year at the top. In fact, only the Rolling Stones, Bob Dylan and *The Sound of Music* would dislodge the band from their perch until February 1967.

John Lennon

John Lennon with the Beatles on
Ready Steady Go

The singles charts would allow a glimpse of acts following in the wake of the Beatles, such as the Animals, the Kinks, the Hollies and the Spencer Davis Group.

'Beatlemania' was the term coined to describe the screaming young girls who lost control every time the Beatles were mentioned. They were allowed to run riot by the older generation, which considered the clean-cut Beatles image to be an acceptable influence. The band's appearance on the 1963 Royal Variety Show sealed the approval of the nation, complete with Lennon's cheeky dig at the audience: 'The people in the cheap seats clap your hands. All the rest of you, if you'll just rattle your jewellery'. It was the sort of comment that made press interviews with the Beatles a joy for everyone. They were led in this by John, whose humour and intelligence made him good copy on any subject, and he had some effect in making rock music thought of as more than a last chance for high school drop-outs. The leap of 'I Want to Hold Your Hand' to number one in America was a unique event for a group which had not laid foot in the country, and in February 1964 the band left to claim their crown. The scenes at the airports, on the *Ed Sullivan Show* and at the concerts completed a bloodless revolution, with viewing figures of almost 74 million for the television appearance, and gigs at which the screaming was louder than the music. By April they held the top five positions in the American singles chart.

They followed their triumph with *A Hard Day's Night*, a film which may have been planned merely as a vehicle for the soundtrack, but which was successful in its own right. The album also gained an audience beyond that of the screaming teens, as the Lennon/McCartney partnership showed a depth way beyond the usually crass songwriting efforts of teen idols. Their musical collage fashioned something totally new out of just about every influential sound flying through the ether – 'The greatest composers since Beethoven', declared the *Sunday Times*. From then on, self-penned compositions would become the norm for artists who had formerly been a showcase for the talents of others.

Later in 1964, the band undertook a
world tour which repeated endlessly
the format of ecstatic crowds, constant
police protection, and orgies which
belied the impression of their public
image. In between their three hits of
the year they left room for songs by
Cilla Black, Manfred Mann and Her-
man's Hermits, for example, to get to
the top of the singles charts. Lennon
became a best-selling author with his
books *John Lennon in His Own Write*
and *A Spaniard in the Works*, and the
band released *Beatles for Sale*. By 1965
the Beatles could do no wrong, and
Lennon found that uncouth public
displays just bounced off the image
that had been manufactured for him.
'Help' and 'Nowhere Man' are exam-
ples of his attempts to describe the

pressure in song, and the albums *Rubber Soul* and *Revolver* witnessed his efforts to define himself with lyrics that left behind the straightforward love-songs of the earlier albums. He had bought a mock-Tudor mansion near Weybridge, but used very few of its many rooms. After the rigours of touring which had continued until September 1965, he almost hibernated there, getting stoned and playing with expensive toys and cars. He felt an emptiness that could not be filled by his family, for his relationship with Cynthia and Julian was minimal, and he turned to the first of many alternatives. He had tried LSD several times before, but now attempted a serious examination of its powers.

Lennon's ironic sense of humour and his natural tendency to speak his mind were an explosive mixture to add to the self-knowledge that LSD claims for its users. It probably had a hand in his remark, in an interview in March 1966, that the Beatles were more popular than Jesus. The God-fearing American public took the comment at face value, and Lennon's apology did no good at the beginning of a tour of the States in August. That year the Beatles had already received death threats in Japan, and a physical beating as they left the Philippines after Epstein had turned down an audience with Imelda Marcos. They received more threats during their dates in the Southern States, and by the end of the tour had decided never to do another.

Lennon signs autographs in Paris

John and Cynthia Lennon

Lennon went straight into the filming of Richard Lester's film *How I Won the War* in Germany and Spain, leaving Britain to the hit song of another Liverpool son, Ken Dodd and 'Tears'. John returned to continue his LSD journey in London, where, on 9 November 1966, he met artist Yoko Ono at an avant-garde exhibition at the Indica Gallery. Ono had rejected the possibilities open to her as a member of a wealthy Japanese family, choosing to live the creative life in New York. Her artistic credibility was not high amongst its prominent movers; but, like the master of the scene, Andy Warhol, she could seize the opportunity when it arose, and, like Lennon, she was adept at creating from a lucky dip of influences. She was in London visiting a series of exhibitions with her husband

Tony Cox and daughter Kyoko, but she decided that Lennon was for her, and John was soon infatuated. Although there are differing accounts of their life together, it seems that they were inseparable within a short time of their meeting.

1967 was the high point of the flower-power movement, the year of Procol Harem's 'A Whiter Shade Of Pale' and Scott McKenzie's 'San Francisco'. The Beatles' album of that year, *Sergeant Pepper and His Lonely Hearts Club Band,* became the monument of the era. Its technology and formulation gave it a unique place in the history of rock music, thanks to George Martin, but by now the driving force of the Beatles was Paul McCartney. John Lennon had never had the patience for drawn-out recording sessions, and Paul was much better able to handle the complications that six months of recording entailed. John did not just sit back, though, being responsible for 'Strawberry Fields Forever', 'Lucy in the Sky with Diamonds' and the single at the centre of the *Sergeant Pepper* experience, 'All You Need is Love'. His resentment at Paul's dominance was a feature of a general frustration within the band, but it was probably McCartney's lead that kept them together at the time. John's drug-use made him a more friendly participant at parties and in the clubs that summer, and he cut a fine, paisley-clad figure driving around in his garishly painted Rolls-Royce.

With George Harrison's encourage-
ment, the band came under the influence of the Maharishi Mahesh Yogi and
his anti-materialist teaching, and John
was very taken with its promise of inner
fulfilment. On 27 August 1967 they
were with him in Bangor in the middle
of a five-day course, when word came
of Brian Epstein's death, apparently by
suicide. Since the Beatles had become
studio-based they needed less of his
time, and his other businesses were
not going so well, although he had
cut himself in for a good percentage
of his main band. Lennon was cut up
by the loss of another influential person
in his life, and turned to Yoko Ono for
support.

1967's other main project was the *Magical Mystery Tour*, which contained Lennon's 'I Am The Walrus', an overt Lewis Carroll reference and a prime example of John's writing through a filtering of the everyday. The film would première on television late in the year, and was the first Beatles product to be less than critically acclaimed. During its making, John was reconciled with his father, Freddie. The two had met several times since 1964, but John had been unable to forgive Freddie for abandoning his family, until the complications were explained to him by his uncle. John bought a house in Brighton for Freddie and his new bride Pauline, and their meetings were, for the most part, friendly.

John and Cynthia were living almost
separate lives by now, but they travelled
together on a Beatles trip to the Maharishi's ashram in India in February 1968.
The holy man's dubious morals were
exposed during their stay and the party
escaped immediately, scuppering the
guru's plans to star with the band on
an American television show. Although
the sojourn had produced a new bag of
songs, Lennon was cured of this parti-
cular spirituality.

He sank back into his drug-taking,
sending the family off to Greece and
secluding himself with his childhood
friend Pete Shotton. By the time
Cynthia returned, John had decided
to make his relationship with Yoko
public, beginning with a symbolic

acorn-planting at the National Sculpture Exhibition at Coventry Cathedral in June 1968, which gave the press a cynical advantage for reports about the woman who had stolen the Beatle. They spent a 'honeymoon' period at Ringo's flat, which had a prize-winning drug pedigree, having been wrecked at one time by a previous occupant, Jimi Hendrix. Lennon had added heroin to his shopping-list during 1967, hanging out with Brian Jones and Keith Richard, and he and Yoko spent nearly a month at the flat, living on champagne, caviare and heroin. They emerged, bound close by chemical as well as physical dependence, for a Lennon art exhibition which displayed obvious Ono influences. When Yoko became pregnant in September 1968,

Cynthia was given the upper hand in the ongoing divorce case, and by November she had a settlement of £100,000 with a trust fund for Julian – Yoko's husband got a much better deal in his divorce.

Taking over from the Hollies' *Greatest Hits*, the Beatles album of 1968 was simply called *The Beatles*, but is always known as the 'White Album'. Featuring many of the songs that had been written in India, it was a bag of individual numbers brought out under the band name, and remains an eclectic and impressive work, though it indicates the fragmentation of the band. The single 'Hey Jude/Revolution' was the first release on Apple Records, the recording arm of Apple Corps, the company that the band formed to control their business affairs, and through which they attempted to develop new artists like James Taylor and Mary Hopkin. At the same time, John and Yoko brought out *Two Virgins*. The cover picture of the naked couple caused much more comment than its contents, an avant-garde collection of noises and sounds which was banned in America. The release was followed on 18 October by John and Yoko's arrest for drug-possession.

Despite a rapid clean-up after a tip-off, small amounts of various drugs were bound to be discovered in the thorough search that the police made. Two weeks later Yoko suffered a miscarriage, though John recorded the foetus' final heartbeats, which were included on 'Life with the Lions'. A week after that they were in court, where Lennon pleaded guilty for fear that Yoko would be deported if they fought the case. He received a fine of £150 and a threat of imprisonment if he was caught again. He had managed to crack the image he had been beating at for so long, but dispelling one myth didn't fill the emptiness he so often seemed to feel at his core.

Poster for the film *Help*

The Beatles advertise their beliefs

John and Yoko Move On

At the beginning of 1969 the Beatles began work on *Let It Be*, which would end up being released after *Abbey Road*. There was disruption caused by an attempt to film them at work as part of their commitment to another cinema project, and also by the presence of Yoko, who, unlike the partners of the other Beatles, insisted on being present in the studio. John tried to insist on a record free of studio technology, wanting a revivalist sound to accompany some of the early numbers they were readdressing, but it was asking the impossible of a group who no longer had the tightness that comes from regular live shows. In a final fit, they took the gear to the flat roof of the studio and played a memorable live set, to the delight of the crowd which gathered in the street below.

The differences between the band opened into hostility over the question of management. Paul put forward his intended father-in-law, music-business lawyer Lee Eastman, as a candidate, but John preferred the choice of Allen Klein, accountant and Rolling Stones' manager. George and Ringo sided with John, and a row during a meeting with the two hopefuls caused the McCartney block to walk out, in the start of a feud. Paul agreed eventually to have Klein investigate their financial situation, which was shown to be dire.

Brian Epstein's work in launching and presenting the Beatles had been vital; but, in almost every area of business, he had sold them short, from the original record and publishing deals, to tax, touring and merchandising. The band was able to access a tiny percentage of its worth, and much of what it had lost was gone for ever. What must have rankled especially was the loss of the rights on about 200 songs to Sir Lew Grade's ATV company. The emotional loss must have been hard enough, and the songs' possible financial worth was borne out by their purchase by Michael Jackson in 1986 for $47.5 million. As a result of his work, Klein got the management deal with the Beatles on a three-to-one vote and successfully renegotiated several areas, most importantly the poor royalty rate.

While the business affairs were coming to light during March 1969, John and Yoko got married on a whim, going to Gibraltar for an instant ceremony. They followed the event with the first of the bed-ins, at the Amsterdam Hilton, in a public advertisement for peace – not, as the invited journalists first presumed, to watch a Beatle give some kind of sex-show. John took to the new cause as energetically as he had his other attempts towards personal growth, and he was

John Lennon and Yoko Ono made their
relationship public in 1968

John and Yoko in New York

rewarded with worldwide coverage of his promotion, with its 'Give peace a chance' banner. The media treatment gave the pair kudos with the anti-war groups, and a welcome diversion from the less savoury press that they had been receiving of late. They followed it with a 'bag-stunt' in Vienna, where they appeared before the press inside a closed-up bed-cover, with its statement against prejudice through visual stereotyping.

Their new identity as artists of controversy and promotion was described in Lennon's song from the time, 'The Ballad of John and Yoko', and they proceeded to Toronto in May for another bed-in and the recording of 'Give Peace a Chance' with a group of celebrities and fans in their hotel bedroom. By then John had taken the name 'Ono' as a marital gesture to Yoko, who disliked the chauvinism of being 'Mrs Lennon'. It was also an opportunity for John to drop the patriotic 'Winston', although technically he could not lose it.

The pressing need to work on *Abbey Road* caused the Lennons' return to England. They preceded it with a trip to Scotland with Julian and Kyoko, where John had spent the happiest times of his youth at his aunt's sheep-croft. Thanks to John's erratic driving he crashed the car, causing facial injuries to himself and Yoko, and they were patched up by the local hospital. The guilty white Austin Maxi was brought back to the new home, Tittenhurst Park, outside Sunningdale, and displayed on a concrete plinth in front of the living-room as a memorial to a narrow escape.

Another consequence was the sight of a large bed in the recording studio, where Yoko continued her recuperation while being able to monitor John's work. The result, released in September 1969 and displacing Blind Faith's eponymous album from the top spot, was a polished, professional album containing Lennon's 'Come Together', which he was very happy with, and the second side's cleverly joined medley of McCartney-influenced technology, which John disdained.

The same month, John and Yoko flew to Toronto as the result of a last minute agreement to play at a rock 'n' roll revival show promising Little Richard, Gene Vincent and Chuck Berry. John's agreement to appear saved the undersold gig from folding, and his arrival with Eric Clapton, bassist Klaus Voorman and drummer Alan White marked the first showing of the Plastic Ono Band. Lennon was very proud of the success of the scratch band, and used it as an impetus to announce to the Beatles that he was finished with them. He was persuaded to delay a public announcement, for the new financial footing that Klein had prepared was dependent upon the success of album sales, which could be put into jeopardy by an official split of the band.

In October Yoko was hit by another miscarriage. John was sure that drug-use was responsible for the failure of Yoko's pregnancies, and attempted to dry out during a boat-trip around Greece. Their return was marked by the *Wedding Album*, a collection of souvenirs accompanying an album of screaming and a press interview, and Lennon's return of his MBE to Buckingham Palace 'in protest against Britain's involvement in the Nigeria-Biafra thing, against our support of the American troops in Vietnam and against 'Cold Turkey' slipping down the charts'. Apart from the 'Cold Turkey' quip, Lennon's gesture was, for him, a serious one. He knew it would get media attention as part of his 'peace offensive', as he had a veteran's knowledge of media tactics and effect. The song 'Cold Turkey' was the searing result of John's attempt to cut himself off from heroin without treatment. It would take an introduction to methadone to have any lasting effect on his habit.

That Christmas, billboards appeared in sites in major cities around the world, declaring 'War is over! If you want it. Happy Christmas from John and Yoko'. A Plastic Ono supergroup including George Harrison, Eric Clapton, Billy Preston and Keith Moon played a 'Peace for Christmas' concert at the Lyceum in London. Announcing plans for a worldwide music and peace conference near Toronto for the following year, Lennon had a meeting with Pierre Trudeau, the Canadian Prime Minister, which confirmed his status as an international presence for his cause. 'The peace thing isn't a gimmick,' he said.

John Lennon's Rolls Royce

John Lennon on stage

'Other people make it a gimmick. Yoko and I are serious.'

In January 1970 the Lennons flew to Alborg, a small town in Denmark, where Tony Cox was living with his new wife and Kyoko, to discuss the unsettled details of Kyoko's custody. John and Cynthia had come to an agreement with regard to Julian, and John was trying to spend time with his son. While they were away, an exhibition of John's lithographs in London was raided by the police, who confiscated half of the works on grounds of indecency. Sales of his pictures of course went up as a result of the publicity, and a court case in April 1970 would decide in favour of the gallery. The Lennons returned from Denmark with their hair shorn. They swopped the hair for a pair of Muhammad Ali's blood-stained boxing shorts, planning to auction them in the cause of peace. John also declared that all future proceeds from his songs would go towards world peace. The proposed Toronto festival collapsed in arguments over money and organization, as John created, recorded and released 'Instant Karma' in ten days. He sang the Phil Spector-produced song on *Top of the Pops* in February, but did not knock Edison Lighthouse's 'Love Grows (Where My Rosemary Goes)' from the top.

Just before the May release of the album *Let It Be* provided a gap in the long chart-supremacy of Simon and Garfunkel's *Bridge over Troubled Water*, Paul

McCartney announced his retirement from the Beatles. The shock-wave went around the world, but John had mentally left the group long before; the formal disbandment merely allowed him to proceed in his new direction with strength from the fact that there was nothing to look back to. A development in his forward momentum was a willingness to confront the terrors of his childhood. Arthur Janov's Primal Scream therapy taught that, by focusing on disturbances in earlier life and literally screaming them away, the psychological wounds which affected adult life could be healed. It was a tailor-made theory for Lennon, and he leaped onto its possibilities in the same way that he had his drug and spiritual enthusiasms. He and Yoko underwent a four-month course at the Institute in California, and the results were offered up in the self-conscious honesty of songs on the *John Lennon/Plastic Ono Band* album of December 1970; the new decade witnessed a new John Lennon in the deeply personal 'Mother' and the rejection of pressures of the past in 'God'. 'It was the most important thing that happened to me', he said of Primal Therapy, 'besides meeting Yoko and being born.'

One ugly result of this experience was a showdown with his father, when John berated him for his failures as a parent, and sent him from the house. They would not talk again until Freddie was on his deathbed, and John regretted that they had not made up properly. Another, more public, outburst occurred in a *Rolling Stone* interview covering two issues in January/February 1971, when Lennon derided the Beatles and the sixties, declaring that the world was still the same, unfair place that it had been before: 'Nothing happened except we all dressed up.'

New York

The Lennons' preoccupations in 1971 lasted for several years. Firstly, there was the division of the Beatles. The animosity between John and Paul grew during the year, and was made public in press interviews. Paul seemed to be belittling John's activities, and John hit back with ferocity, culminating in the vinyl dismembering of 'How Do You Sleep?' on *Imagine*. McCartney's application to the courts for the resolution of the Beatles'

John and Yoko with Julian Lennon

The Dakota Building, near New York's Central Park

finances provoked the holding of any future royalties in a fund from which the four were allowed to draw an allowance. This arrangement continued until the matter was finalized in 1975.

Secondly, there was family, with the continuing conflict over custody of Kyoko, aged eight. Tony Cox had disappeared with the child, and surfaced in Majorca. John and Yoko flew there, and, on 23 April, Allen Klein was contacted with the news that they were being held by the police after Tony Cox reported Kyoko missing from a playground. Cox slipped off the island, while Klein managed to get the Lennons freed without charge. They heard that Cox was in New York, and John was successful in obtaining a nine-month visa from June to search for Kyoko. This marked John's introduction to the city which became the Liverpool of his last decade, one in which he felt at ease as an artist, and not like a 'guy who won the pools'.

Thirdly, there was art. A series of John's avant-garde films was shown in Cannes and London during the year. In *Erection*, the construction of a building over eighteen months was filmed through still-photos of the work. In *Apotheosis*, a camera was attached to a helium balloon which rose into the clouds, becoming a long visual white-out. The climax for John and Yoko was her exhibition at the Everson Museum of Fine Art in New York, 'This Is Not Here'. A hastily put together project in a massive space, its centre-piece, the 'Water Event', featured one hundred donations by artists and celebrities on a water theme. John's gift was a pink object inside a plastic bag labelled 'Napoleon's Bladder'. Unfortunately, the exhibition was trashed by an invasion of fans who wanted to see John Lennon. 'What was meant to be was meant to be,' said Yoko.

Imagine, the best-known of Lennon's solo albums, was recorded in the studio that he had set up at Tittenhurst and at the Record Plant in New York during July, and was released in October. Its commercial sound was topped with the plaintive simplicity of the title track, and was a welcome relief to the fans who had been confused by the harshness of his recent work. The film *Imagine*, which followed the album, was an arty profile of John and Yoko, memorable for the beauty of the Tittenhurst-shot scenes accompanying the title track.

By this time, they had settled permanently in New York. John immersed himself in the area around Greenwich Village, with guides in streetwise busker David Peel, for whose album John would be producer, and, occasionally, Bob Dylan. Part of John's association with the area was an involvement with its left-wing radicals, led by Jerry Rubin. The Lennons appeared at a rally in support of the jailed White Panther leader, John Sinclair, and at other political demonstrations. John was thus brought to the attention of the

Flowers for John Lennon at the place where
he was shot

Yoko Ono with Sean

Immigration Services, who ordered his deportation after the expiry of his visa in February 1972. The pretext was Lennon's 1968 drug conviction, but the fear was that he was involved in a proposed disruption of the 1972 Republican Convention, and the political statements of his June 1972 album, *Some Time in New York City*, did not ease the nerves of a troubled and suspicious administration. Lennon's four-year battle for a green card would include his being watched, followed, and phone-tapped by the FBI to a degree which did not equate with the reason given for his deportation. As a result, Lennon would be unable to leave America until 1976 for fear that he would not be allowed back in. A plus for the public was a profile-raising benefit for handicapped children that he played at Madison Square Gardens in August 1972.

As though he didn't have enough problems to deal with going into 1973, Lennon decided to drop the management services of Allen Klein, who brought out a lawsuit for unrepaid loans. For most of the year Lennon hibernated at home, which had become the Dakota Building in Manhattan, and he started work on the album *Mind Games*. He dealt with the pressures of life by relying on drink and drugs, and the resulting strain on his seemingly impregnable relationship with Yoko snapped it in the autumn. He began an eighteen-month period known as the 'Lost Weekend', leaving for Los Angeles with his secretary, May Pang,

when Yoko kicked him out. Yoko
condoned the eventual relationship between John and May Pang; she knew
that he had never been without a
partner, and considered that one who
relied on her for a salary was an obvious
preference to an independent woman.
May Pang was a steady, non-drug-tak-
ing girl, who nevertheless could put little
restraint on what became a return to the
wild days of John's youth. It might well
have been a necessary exorcism for a
man who tried in many ways to address
the demons within him, but it was a
trying time for many of the people he
came into contact with. He was thrown
out of the Troubadour Club after a
drunken swearing match, and smashed
up the Bel Air house that record producer Lou Adler had lent him, forcing

his friends to tie him to a bed to stop the mayhem.

He had gathered a select group of musicians to record a rock 'n' roll covers album produced by Phil Spector, and the sessions dissolved into drunkenness and arguments between star and producer. *Mind Games* was released in the middle of the sessions, and its professional sound must have made Lennon even more frustrated by the lack of progress. A final abortive session before Christmas was followed by Spector's disappearance with the master tapes.

Lennon moved into a house with Harry Nilsson, Klaus Voorman, Keith Moon and Ringo Starr, just some of the friends with whom he had been bar-hopping all over the city. During May 1974 John worked on and produced Nilsson's *Pussy Cats*, and this responsibility forced him to slow the pace a little. His alcoholic haze did clear enough for him to produce *Walls And Bridges*, released in October 1974, a beautifully packaged album containing his first number one American single, 'Whatever Gets You through the Night'. As he said of the album, 'I'm almost amazed that I could get anything out . . . It was the work of a semi-sick craftsman.' By this time, Lennon was moving back towards a normal existence. Back in New York in a flat on East 52nd Street, he saw quite a bit of Mick Jagger, for whom he had a lot of respect, and met up with Paul McCartney. As a result of a bet with

Elton John over the chart position of 'Whatever Gets You through the Night' (Elton had said it would be number one), Lennon appeared with him at Elton's Madison Square Gardens concert in November.

By then, Lennon was in negotiations with music publisher Morris Levy over a copyright infringement of the Levy-owned Chuck Berry song 'You Can't Catch Me' on 'Come Together' from *Abbey Road*. John had regained the Phil Spector masters after six months of trying, and, although only three tracks were worth saving, it was agreed that an album based around them would be brought out by Levy's budget mail-order company. Lennon put down ten tracks in just a few days to complete the album. The problem was that they would need a release from EMI to bring the album out. John was talked out of the project by his lawyer, but Levy ignored the dangers, and the illegal *Roots* was on sale from February 1975. The official version, *Rock and Roll*, was rush-released by EMI/Capitol, and Levy's distribution was choked by threats from the powerful major label.

1975 was a year when order was restored. In January the Beatles were officially divorced, and John got back together with Yoko – although she did not let him move in formally until March. He had certainly regained his optimism, and continued his creative form, working with David Bowie on his *Young Americans* album and co-writing Bowie's first American number one, 'Fame'. And finally, soon after their reconciliation, Yoko became pregnant. John had undergone acupuncture to try to increase a low sperm-count, which he believed was due to the amount of drink and drugs he had consumed. He and Yoko had been trying to 'clean up their act', and from the moment the pregnancy was announced he treated her like an invalid, sometimes pushing her around in a wheelchair.

They had agreed, on John's return, that he should have some sort of life outside the Dakota Building, and he would go off to the coast at Montauk; although he might get drunk, he had the stability of the 'dry' Dakota to return to. They had a symbolic second marriage, and agreed that he would take care of the child, allowing Yoko to take over the bread-winning role. John Lennon, held up as a symbol of success and innovation around the world, was determined to be a success at the one thing which had been at the root of so many problems in his life: family. His five-year retirement indicates the strength of his commitment to the ideal.

On 9 October 1975, John's 35th birth-day, and two days after a court's reversal of his deportation order, Yoko gave birth to a son by Caesarean section. The delivery was delicate, and John blew up at a doctor's request for an autograph as Yoko was coming out of sedation. The birth was treated by him as a miracle, and Sean Taro Ono Lennon was treated as such. As a coda to the era, the compilation album *Shaved Fish*, released just after Sean's birth, was a compact résumé of John's recent music, and would be the last that fans would hear of him for five years.

Tragedy

For the next few years, Yoko built up a portfolio of property, buying houses and farms, including a dairy herd, one of which, a Friesian cow, fetched a record $265,000 at auction. 'Only Yoko Ono could sell a cow for a quarter of a million dollars,' joked John. She bought up several of the flats in the Dakota, and a retreat overlooking the Atlantic on Long Island, the only one of their many other residences that the Lennons used regularly. Her business techniques placed great emphasis on the use of astrology and numerology, not usually deemed important in the corporate world. The tarot cards also affected any travel plans – direction and time of journeys being vital for her. Thus the family's yearly trip to Japan might involve them travelling separately and in different directions. Yoko's reliance on such practices made her vulnerable to less than scrupulous characters among psychic practitioners, and some of the artefacts that made their way into the Lennon houses were vastly overpriced 'psychic necessities'.

Lennon allowed Yoko's priorities to take the lead, as he immersed himself in his duties as a house-husband, proudly sending a photo of his first self-baked loaf of bread to his friend Elliot Mintz in California. His devotion to Sean gave him no patience for most of the worldly activities which had taken up his time in the past, and he swamped the boy with expensive toys in a plan of 'over-materialization', to give Sean a disregard of such things. He was an unsuccessful student of Japanese, and took several unnoticed trips around the world – he would delight in his anonymity, until, of course, he handed over a credit card.

In the first half of 1976 John was stricken by the deaths of his father, one of his aunts, and the tragic killing of Beatles retainer Mal Evans, and he believed himself to be marked out for an early death. He managed to accommodate his continued weakness for drugs with a strict health regime which made him noticeably thin. But he finally grew closer to Julian, now aged thirteen, teaching him to play the guitar and spending time with him on holiday.

He disliked most of the rock music of the late 1970s, and he took to listening to music from earlier in the century, especially Bing Crosby. Yoko gave him a Wurlitzer which played only 78r.p.m. records for his thirty-eighth birthday.

In August 1980 Lennon's love of the sea was fulfilled by an ocean voyage from Rhode Island to Bermuda with a five-man crew. The rough seas that they encountered gave Lennon a new sense of himself, and his safe arrival sparked off a fit of songwriting, news of which was flashed around the world. Yoko had also been writing again, and the couple agreed to share an album. John got some musicians together – for an occasion like this he could take his pick of the crop – and he recorded over twenty songs with a speed which impressed all around him. The publicity campaign was headed by an interview for *Playboy* magazine, and the label of release was to be the recently formed Geffen Records, because owner David Geffen was willing to take the record without hearing it.

Double Fantasy was released on 17 November 1980, a double album showcasing John's emotional stability in the lyrical maturity of '(Just Like) Starting

Over' and 'Woman', and the long-term influence of the 1950s in the treatment of his recorded voice. He had just celebrated his fortieth birthday, and was feeling ready to capitalize on his rediscovered muse with more writing. Though thin, and due to undergo an operation for the rebuilding of his drug-damaged nose, he was displaying an energy that no one could deny; and, despite only lukewarm critical reviews for the album, there was a general excitement about the prospect of his potential in the 1980s.

Everything was brought to a sudden and tragic stop at 10.50 p.m. on 8 December (the early morning of the 9th in the UK). Twenty-five-year-old Mark Chapman, Lennon fan and born-again

Christian, who had got Lennon to autograph a copy of *Double Fantasy* earlier that day, put four bullets into John's back as he returned from the studio. John died at the Roosevelt Hospital, within a short time of being rushed there by the first policemen to arrive at the scene. The world mourned, and Yoko retreated for several days in the Dakota, where a quarter of a million letters of sympathy would arrive during the next two months.

The shock of the killing had an immediate effect on a whole generation, which realized what Lennon had meant to it. The obvious result of his death would be the number one chart position for Lennon material, new and old. The symbol of John Lennon's influence was the ten minutes' silence joined by millions around the world, led by over 100,000 people in Central Park, on 14 December, 1980, four days after his cremation at Hartsdale Crematorium, New York. They were all acknowledging the inspiration of a man who put his unique life and search for growth into a form which has affected popular music to this day. We cannot even guess at what he might have achieved if he had been allowed to live a full life.

FURTHER MINI SERIES
INCLUDE

THEY DIED TOO YOUNG

Elvis
James Dean
Buddy Holly
Jimi Hendrix
Sid Vicious
Marc Bolan
Ayrton Senna
Marilyn Monroe
Jim Morrison

THEY DIED TOO YOUNG

Malcolm X
Kurt Cobain
River Phoenix
John Lennon
Glenn Miller
Isadora Duncan
Rudolph Valentino
Freddie Mercury
Bob Marley

FURTHER MINI SERIES
INCLUDE

HEROES OF THE WILD WEST

General Custer
Butch Cassidy and the Sundance Kid
Billy the Kid
Annie Oakley
Buffalo Bill
Geronimo
Wyatt Earp
Doc Holliday
Sitting Bull
Jesse James